VIOLIN SOLO · PIANO

THE GREATEST SHOWMAN

MEDLEY FOR VIOLIN AND PIANO

ARRANGED BY

T0081641

ISBN 978-1-5400-2756-6

7777 W. BLUEMOUND RD. P.O. BOX 13819 MILWAUKEE, WI 53213

In Australia Contact:
Hal Leonard Australia Pty. Ltd.
4 Lentara Court
Cheltenham, Victoria, 3192 Australia
Email: ausadmin@halleonard.com.au

Visit Hal Leonard Online at
www.halleonard.com

THE GREATEST SHOWMAN MEDLEY

Words and Music by BENJ PASEK
and JUSTIN PAUL
Arranged by LINDSEY STIRLING
Piano arrangement by DAVID RUSSELL
and JENNIFER STIRLING

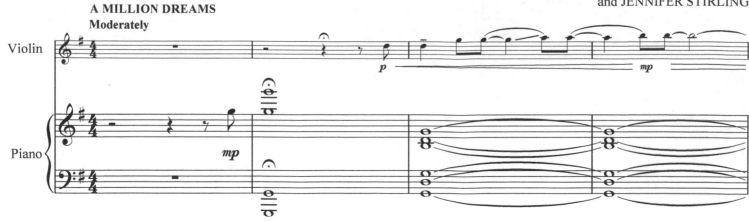

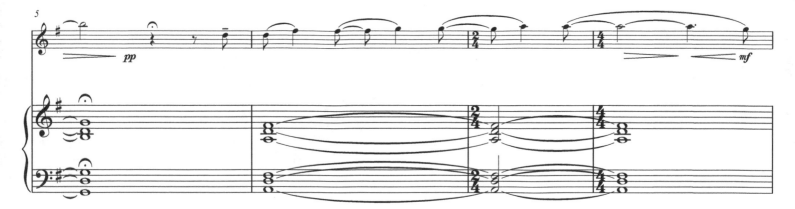

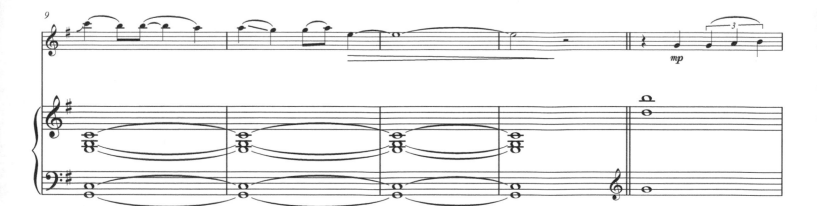

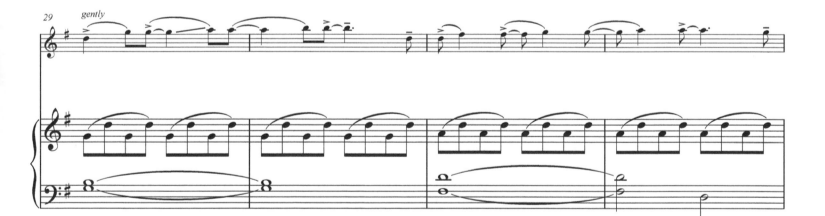

NEVER ENOUGH

THE GREATEST SHOWMAN

MEDLEY FOR VIOLIN AND PIANO

ARRANGED BY

ISBN 978-1-5400-2756-6

HAL•LEONARD®

7777 W. BLUEMOUND RD. P.O. BOX 13819 MILWAUKEE, WI 53213

In Australia Contact:
Hal Leonard Australia Pty. Ltd.
4 Lentara Court
Cheltenham, Victoria, 3192 Australia
Email: ausadmin@halleonard.com.au

Visit Hal Leonard Online at
www.halleonard.com

HL00276951

THE GREATEST SHOWMAN MEDLEY

Words and Music by BENJ PASEK
and JUSTIN PAUL
Arranged by LINDSEY STIRLING
Piano arrangement by DAVID RUSSELL
and JENNIFER STIRLING

A MILLION DREAMS
Moderately

NEVER ENOUGH

3

gently, with ease

with determination

REWRITE THE STARS

with determination

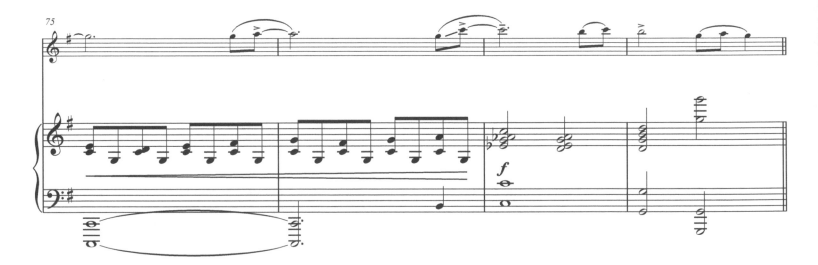

REWRITE THE STARS

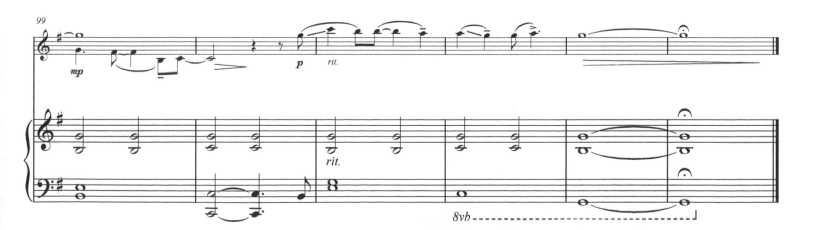